A Note to Parents

DK READERS is a compelling program for beginning readers, designed in conjunction with leading literacy experts, including Dr. Linda Gambrell, Distinguished Professor of Education at Clemson University. Dr. Gambrell has served as President of the National Reading Conference, the College Reading Association, and the International Reading Association.

Beautiful illustrations and superb full-color photographs combine with engaging, easy-to-read stories to offer a fresh approach to each subject in the series. Each DK READER is guaranteed to capture a child's interest while developing his or her reading skills, general knowledge, and love of reading.

The five levels of DK READERS are aimed at different reading abilities, enabling you to choose the books that are exactly right for your child:

Pre-level 1: Learning to read
Level 1: Beginning to read
Level 2: Beginning to read alone
Level 3: Reading alone
Level 4: Proficient readers

The "normal" age at which a child begins to read can be anywhere from three to eight years old. Adult participation through the lower levels is very helpful for providing encouragement, discussing storylines, and sounding out unfamiliar words.

No matter which level you select, you can be sure that you are helping your child learn to read, then read to learn!

LONDON, NEW YORK, MUNICH,
MELBOURNE, AND DELHI

Series Editor Deborah Lock
Senior Art Editor Tory Gordon-Harris
U.S. Editor Elizabeth Hester
Design Assistant Sadie Thomas
Jacket Designer Natalie Godwin
Production Siu Chan
DTP Designer Almudena Díaz
Art Director Rachael Foster
Publishing Manager Bridget Giles

Reading Consultant
Linda Gambrell, Ph.D.

First American edition, 2003
This edition, 2009
10 11 12 13 10 9 8 7 6 5 4 3 2
Published in the United States by DK Publishing
375 Hudson Street, New York, New York 10014

Published in Great Britain by Dorling Kindersley Limited.

DK books are available at special discounts when purchased
in bulk for sales promotions, premiums,
fund-raising, or educational use.
For details, contact: DK Publishing Special Markets
375 Hudson Street, New York, New York 10014
SpecialSales@dk.com

A catalog record for this book is available
from the Library of Congress

ISBN: 978-0-7566-5601-0 (pb)
ISBN: 978-0-7566-5602-7 (plc)

Color reproduction by Colourscan, Singapore
Printed and bound in China by L. Rex Printing Co. Ltd.

The publisher would like to thank the following for
their kind permission to reproduce their photographs:
a=above; c=center; b=below; l=left; r=right t=top;

Ardea London Ltd: 18-19; **Corbis**: Stephen Frink 16-17; Jeffrey
L. Rotman 26-27; **Getty Images**: AEF - Tony Malquist 12t, 28c;
Pete Atkinson 2-3; David Fleetham/Visuals Limited, Inc. 10-11, 20tl;
Jeff Hunter 6-7, 30-31; Herwarth Voigtmann 4-5t; **Nature Picture
Library Ltd**: Constantino Petrinos 23tr; **N.H.P.A.**: Pete Atkinson
14-15; **Science Photo Library**: GUSTO 4l.
Jacket: Getty Images: Stuart Westmorland front.

All other images © Dorling Kindersley
For further information see: www.dkimages.com

Discover more at
www.dk.com

DK READERS

LEARNING TO READ pre-level 1

Fishy Tales

DK Publishing

Take a
swim in the
blue sea.

snorkel

clam

Here is a
coral reef.

 coral

What do you see?

fish

coral

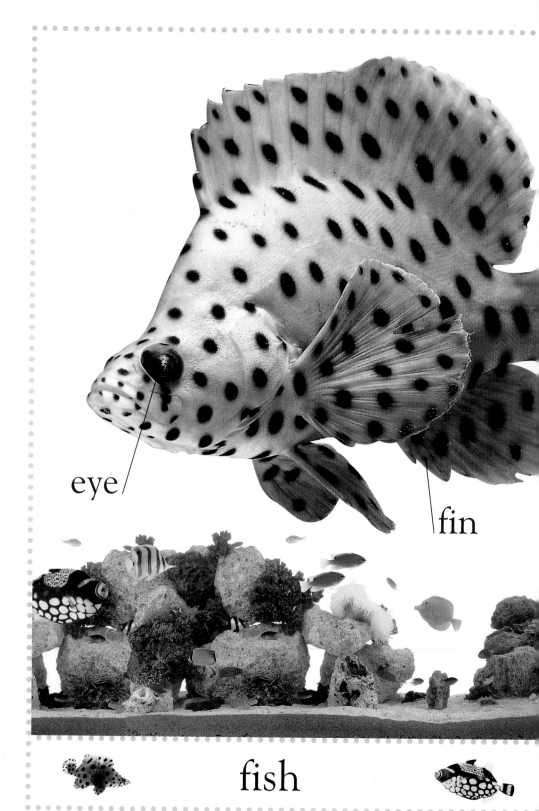

eye

fin

fish

spot

Small fish
swim in
and out of
the coral.

The turtles play in the sea.

shell

 turtles

flipper

tail

sea horses

fin

snout

The sea horses
sway to and fro.

arm

 starfish

Starfish crawl
on the sea floor.

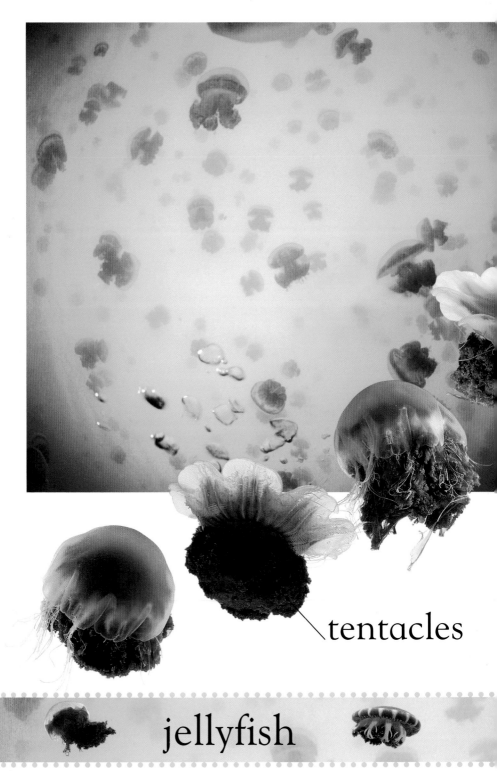

tentacles

jellyfish

Jellyfish
float up
and down
in the sea.

bell

fin

tail

Here comes a shark.
It looks for food.

sharks

mouth

octopuses

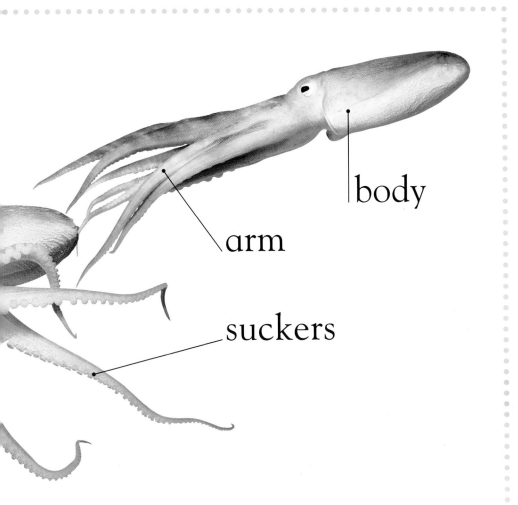

body

arm

suckers

An octopus
shoots off
to hide.

claw

crabs

leg

Crabs hide in
the coral and
in big shells.

shell

tail

A ray hides on
the sea floor.

rays

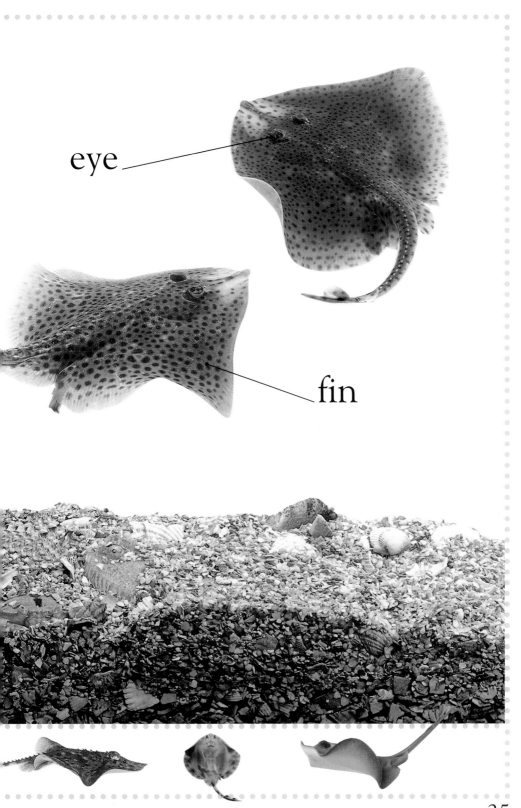

eye

fin

A dolphin swims
away from
the shark.

mouth

dolphins

tail

flipper

Eels look out for the shark.

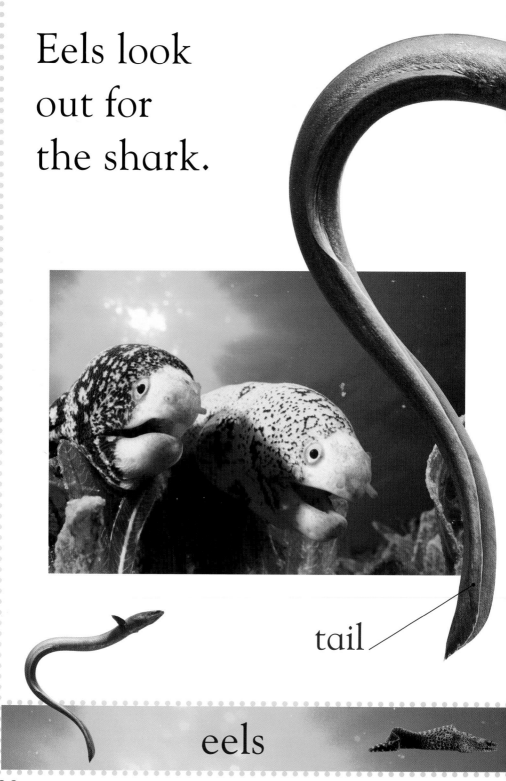

tail

eels

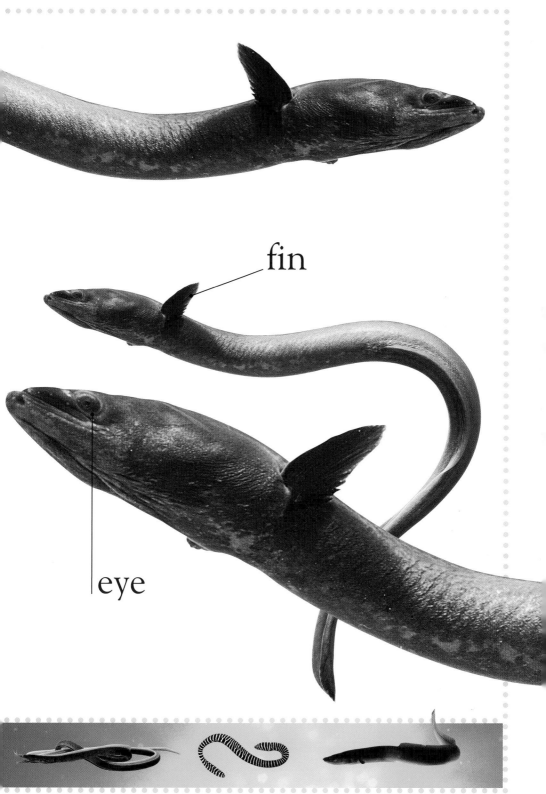

fin

eye

The shark
swims away.

 Can you see ...